Good Housekeeping
Cookery Club

*Q*UICK COOKING

TED SMART

A TED SMART Publication 1995

1 3 5 7 9 10 8 6 4 2

First published in the United Kingdom in 1994 by Ebury Press
Random House, 20 Vauxhall Bridge Road, London SW1V 2SA

Random House Australia (Pty) Limited
20 Alfred Street, Milsons Point, Sydney,
New South Wales 2061, Australia

Random House New Zealand Limited
18 Poland Road, Glenfield,
Auckland 10, New Zealand

Random House South Africa (Pty) Limited
PO Box 337, Bergvlei, South Africa

Random House UK Limited Reg. No. 954009

A CIP catalogue record for this book is available from the British Library.

Managing Editor: JANET ILLSLEY
Design: SARA KIDD
Special Photography: KEN FIELD
Food Stylist: LOUISE PICKFORD
Photographic Stylist: SUZY GITTINS
Techniques Photography: KARL ADAMSON
Food Techniques Stylist: ANGELA KINGSBURY
Recipe Testing: EMMA-LEE GOW

ISBN 0 09 180544 9

Typeset in Gill Sans by Textype Typesetters, Cambridge
Colour Separations by Magnacraft, London
Printed and bound in Italy by New Interlitho Italia S.p.a., Milan

CONTENTS

COOKERY NOTES

- Both metric and imperial measures are given for the recipes. Follow either metric or imperial throughout as they are not interchangeable.
- All spoon measures are level unless otherwise stated. Sets of measuring spoons are available in both metric and imperial sizes for accurate measurement of small quantities.
- If a stage is specified under freezing instructions, the dish should be frozen at the end of that stage.

- Ovens should be preheated to the specified temperature. Grills should also be preheated. The cooking times given in the recipes assume that this has been done.
- Size 2 eggs should be used except where otherwise specified. Free-range eggs are recommended.
- Use freshly ground black pepper unless otherwise specified.
- Use fresh rather than dried herbs unless dried herbs are suggested in the recipe.

INTRODUCTION

All home cooks are workers, whether they go out to their workplace or dash about all day delivering and collecting children hither and yon in between keeping things ticking over in good order on the home front. We all juggle multiple activities, and only professional chefs can devote long hours to the meticulous planning and immaculate preparation of dinner. That's what they are paid to do, and we domestic cooks are not. We do it for love!

We cook because we like to – or at least because we appreciate good food. If we didn't, we could all rely entirely on the microwave and ever-increasing ranges of fresh and frozen ready-made meals from the supermarket. With the occasional bag of ready-washed and torn-up salad leaves, we'd stay reasonably healthy without ever touching a cook's knife or a saucepan, and the supermarkets would rejoice in ever fatter profits. There's nothing intrinsically immoral about choosing not to cook – not even for women!

But the fact that you have bought this book, or that someone knows you well enough to have given it to you, suggests that you do find joy in the preparation of good food. You gain some elemental satisfaction from the handling of raw ingredients, and real reward in offering the fruits of your creativity to those you most love, be they friends or family.

So to our stoves. We won't be there for long, so let's enjoy it. No single dish in this book takes more than three-quarters of an hour to prepare from start to finish, and if that's the main course, we could be sitting down to the starter within half an hour of putting the key in the door. There may be a few minutes' pause between courses, but what's the rush? Surely a meal can take as long to eat as it does to get ready, unless the cook's time and effort are being seriously under-valued.

Many of today's fashionable ingredients lend themselves perfectly to quick and easy dishes. Fish cooks almost instantly, and supermarket fresh fish counters are now competing with traditional fishmongers to win customers by offering full preparation services. Small lean cuts of meat can be fast grilled or flash-fried, and larger pieces, properly trimmed, will roast in a hot oven within our prescribed short time limit. Rice and pasta cook quickly and are open to endless variations, while leafy vegetables and baby vegetables need almost no time to cook.

You don't have to start from scratch with every course: your starter might be a pleasingly garnished platter of charcuterie or some smoked fish; a salad of sliced tomatoes and shredded basil dressed with good oil and served with fancy shop-bought bread; ready-made soup from a can or carton, also offered with interesting bread; a ready-made pâté; or a special seasonal vegetable, like asparagus, served simply topped with melted butter and fresh herbs.

Cheese or yogurt and fresh fruit make a fine finish on most days, and homemade puddings should be regarded as something of a treat. When a sweet ending is called for, choose one of the fast desserts from the final chapter.

On the facing page are selected menus made up from the recipes in this book. Treat them as encouraging suggestions. It's not usually a good idea to tackle three unfamiliar recipes in the same meal, particularly if you are expecting company and likely to be in a rush. But if you like this book as much as I hope you will, favourite recipes from it will become part of your repertoire, cookable from memory, and you can turn to other chapters for new inspiration. Gravy-stained pages are the cookery writer's finest reward!

MENU SUGGESTIONS

ELEGANT MENU FOR 4

Chilled Beetroot and Apple Soup

•

Upper-crust Seared Salmon on Spiced Lentils

•

Peaches with a Hot Zabaglione Sauce

Workplan: Make soup and chill • Prepare peaches • Prepare salmon • Cook lentils and prepare their vegetables • Cook salmon and finish lentils between courses • Make zabaglione sauce just before serving.

INFORMAL MENU FOR 4

Leek and Potato Soup

•

Sausage Coiled in a Cake Tin

•

Pears with a Hot Fudge Sauce

Workplan: Heat oven • Prepare main course, soup vegetables and pears • Bake sausage • Make soup • Make pudding sauce between courses.

SPICY MENU FOR 4

Fattoush

•

Spiced Lamb with Spinach and Potato

•

Dates and Bananas with Scented Cream and Cinnamon

Workplan: Make Fattoush • Prepare dates and cream. Heat grill • Prepare and cook lamb and vegetables; keep warm in oven while serving starter • Slice bananas and assemble pudding between courses.

INSTANT MENU FOR 4

Eggs with Smoked Salmon and Black Pepper

•

Stir-fried King Prawns on Sesame Noodles

•

Bananas Grilled with Cardamom Butter

Workplan: Prepare main course ingredients • Make and serve starter • Cook next courses to order.

STYLISH MENU FOR 4

Pasta and Courgettes in Tomato Cream

•

Poached Trout with Dill and Horseradish Mayonnaise

•

Galettes of Minted Blackcurrants

Workplan: Poach trout • Make mayonnaise • Prepare galettes • Cool and skin trout • Heat oven • Make starter and cook galettes while eating it • Turn off oven and leave door ajar while main course is eaten • Swirl cassis into cream just before serving.

INFORMAL MENU FOR 4

Lockets Savoury

•

Chicken Livers in Mushroom Cups

•

Honey-scented Creams

Workplan: Make soufflé • Prepare main course • Heat oven and grill • Prepare and cook starter • Keep main course warm in oven while serving starter.

GUIDE TO USEFUL INGREDIENTS

Keeping an appropriate range of ingredients to hand will give you plenty of scope for concocting quick, tasty meals effortlessly. The following guide to stocking your storecupboard, freezer and refrigerator with useful ingredients should provide you with plenty of ideas.

THE VEGETABLE STORE

Canned tomatoes are a respected standby even at the late-summer peak of the fresh tomato season. Not only are they ready-prepared for instant convenience, but they pack in the fruity intensity of flavour required for sauce-making. Recent improvements include ready-chopped tomatoes in their own juice, though the addition of dried herbs is a dubious advantage: better to add your own, preferably fresh. Use for soups and pasta sauces, and in casseroles, pies and chilli con carne.

Some pulses withstand canning rather well, and this of course eliminates soaking and long cooking times. Chick peas add chunky texture to rice and grain-based dishes, and purée successfully into dips, such as hummus.

Red kidney beans are an excellent addition to casseroles. The French unapologetically serve canned or bottled pale green flageolets as a vegetable with lamb, so you should certainly feel no embarrassment in following suit – adding some chopped fresh herbs if you can.

Canned pulses – such as flageolets, haricot beans and red kidney beans – combine well with fresh green beans in salads, but remember to rinse them well before use.

Dried mushrooms seem expensive until you rehydrate them to their full vegetable status. They are particularly good in risottos and delicate sauces.

Useful ingredients to keep in the freezer include chopped spinach to serve as an accompanying vegetable, fill omelettes or pancakes, or use as the foundation for Florentine eggs. Frozen peas – particularly petits pois – and broad beans are acceptable emergency vegetables and useful in risottos and rice salads, or mixed with other pulses and fresh herbs in bean salads. Sweetcorn can be served just as it is, or used as the basis of a substantial chowder.

CANNED FISH

Fish such as tuna, anchovies and sardines are more familiar canned than fresh: look for them in oil rather than brine or, as sometimes happens with sardines, in tomato sauce.

Sardines are good as part of a mixed hors d'oeuvre, as a salad starter with tomatoes or cucumber, or mashed into a rough pâté to pile on toast.

Mash anchovies into butter and use as an instant dressing for fish or vegetables, or mix with olive oil, garlic and chilli for a powerful pasta sauce. Partner them with eggs in innumerable starters and supper dishes. Include them in rice salads and Salade Niçoise . . . or eat them plain on well buttered toast.

Tuna makes a good sweetcorn or potato-based chowder, partners beans or hard-boiled eggs in high-protein starters, and is essential to Salade Niçoise. It is also used to fill quiches and omelettes, make sauce for pasta, give substance to rice salads, flake into mashed potato for chunky fish cakes, and mash down into dips . . . don't be caught without a tin.

DRY GOODS

Pasta and rice are the foundation of the storecupboard, and at no time should you have less than two varieties of each in stock, preferably more. The minimum pasta requirement is one long, sleek variety for silkier sauces, and thicker, chunkier shapes – ridged and, or hollow – to hold their own with sturdier sauces containing cream, cheese and meat. This isn't by any means an irreversible rule, but a useful guideline.

Noodles make an ideal quick-cooking accompaniment. Some of the crimped oriental egg noodles that look like unravelled knitting wool simply need to stand in boiling water to soften, and can be laced through with beansprouts and other vegetables and dressing. Wispy vermicelli is similarly fast to cook.

Your need one rice which absorbs its liquid in soft and sloppy style for risotto, and one that stays dry and fluffy for pilaffs and rice salads, and to serve as a starchy accompaniment to generously sauced dishes. The most basic choice would be arborio for the first and long-grain American (easy-cook if you like) for the second purpose, but it is richly rewarding to explore and increase your rice repertoire with other varieties, such

as fragrant basmati. Brown rice takes rather longer to cook but offers higher bulk and nutritional values. Barley cooks in about the same time and makes a comfortingly sticky pilaff, especially good mixed with chick peas and lamb or mushrooms. It also makes a good chewy base for vegetable soups.

Spices are the natural ally of grain-based dishes. Buy little and often, and in as whole a state as is practical: cinnamon sticks, whole nutmeg and star anise, green cardamoms in pods.

Cumin and coriander both keep their flavour longer as seeds than as powder, and are soft and easy to grind – toast them first, shaking them about over a low heat in a dry pan until they release flavour. Buy vanilla pods and store one in a jar of caster sugar to impart a delicate flavour. Use the vanilla-scented sugar to enhance custards, creams, sauces and ice creams.

Pulses that need no prior soaking and cook in only 30-40 minutes also earn a place in the quick cook's store. These include little orange lentils and split green ones for soups and purées. For daintier dishes and salads, use smart Puy lentils which are renowned for their flavour.

JARS OF FLAVOUR

More and more good things come in glass. We have always expected sweet conserves, jams, spreads and honey in jars, but now there are comparable concentrations of savoury flavour to look for too. Pesto can stand on its own as a light sauce for pasta or serve a useful dressing function on vegetables and in soups. Olive pastes, tapenade (olive and anchovy) and Gentleman's Relish (basically anchovy and very savoury) can be slackened with oil to similar purpose.

Sun-dried tomatoes can be bought in oil or, more economically, you can buy them dried and store some or all of them in a jar of olive oil. As the tomatoes soften they will release savoury flavour into the oil, so you should treasure it as a basis for sauces and dressings when you have used the tomatoes. You can work the same trick with olives: buy them loose from delicatessen brine-barrels, then store in a jar of sunflower oil, which will take on an olivey flavour while it preserves your olives.

Capers and mustards are flavouring standbys. Have a smooth Dijon mustard for creamy sauces and a grainy one to give crunch to dressings for vegetables and salads. English mustard, hottest of the lot, is best bought dry and mixed with water a few minutes before it is to be used.

OILS AND VINEGARS

Two oils are the absolute minimum – one fruity olive and one bland vegetable, peanut or sunflower oil. But it is well worth keeping a walnut or hazelnut oil for luxurious dressings, and a jar of powerfully flavoured sesame oil for stir-fries and other oriental dishes. Note that these flavoured oils must be kept in the refrigerator after opening.

Vinegars keep almost indefinitely, so there's no reason not to have a good range to hand: red and white wine vinegar for dressings and to give an acidic lift to soups, stews and sauces; cider vinegar for sweeter dressings suitable for grated salads of winter roots; and balsamic vinegar for the most luxurious of all dressings and finishes. Include rice vinegar if you are keen on oriental cooking, and raspberry vinegar for a summery lift to dressings for salads, avocado, fish and poultry.

BOTTLED SAUCES

Reach for Worcestershire sauce to add depth to meat sauces and to liven up cooked cheese and mushroom dishes. Soy sauce has taken the place of gravy browning for modern cooks, deepening flavour as well as darkening richly, and you can hardly start on an oriental creation without it. Anchovy essence and Tabasco are both useful finishing sauces to give a savoury or chilli-hot lift to dressings. And don't despise tomato ketchup: it can be used to add fruity sweetness to soups and sauces.

HOARDED FRUIT HARVEST

Dried prunes and apricots no longer come like bullets, requiring overnight soaking. In their newer, chewy, rehydrated guise they form a useful storecupboard standby for both savoury and dessert purposes. But as with canned fruits, it's best to mix the preserved with something fresh in compotes or fruit salads. Prunes and oranges are a favourite combination, and dried apricots are good with grapes or soft berries.

Small-grained fruits are the best ones to freeze – especially raspberries, blackberries, red and black currants. Fruits canned in natural juices are usually preferable to those in syrup, though lychees canned in syrup are a useful basis for a winter fruit salad. Use the liquor from the can as a dressing for the salad – sharpening it with citrus juice, or enhancing with ginger wine, a fruity or almondy liqueur or a fragrant dash of rosewater.

For an instant dessert, purée flavourful fresh fruits – such as strawberries or mango – in a food processor, then fold with cream and sweeten to taste, to make a richly flavoured and hearteningly golden fruit fool.

SALADS AND HERBS

The more you rely on the store-cupboard for mainstay ingredients, the more you must turn to salads to provide balancing freshness, and indeed salads are the quick and easy standby of all cooks in a hurry. At its simplest, salad-making involves no more than washing a few leaves, tearing them into a bowl and tossing in a dressing.

In an emergency you can get the supermarket to do the tearing up for you, but on the whole it makes better sense to buy your salads whole, for once torn they soon brown at the edges and can't be stored for long. Also, of course, salad ingredients bought whole are much cheaper, and they generally store well if treated with care. Lettuces from the supermarket are usually clean, and need nothing more than wrapping loosely in a polythene bag and storing in the bottom of the refrigerator. Earthier lettuces should be rinsed and shaken dry before wrapping.

Your choice of salad leaves will be governed by season. In summer it's easy to be seduced by elegantly long and juicy Cos leaves, crisp and curly Webbs and tender round butterhead lettuces. Basic winter salad leaves tend to be more bitter – frilly frisée, batavia and members of the endive family, such as chicory and radicchio. Spinach is always a useful standby, since what doesn't go

SALAD HERBS AND LEAVES
*ABOVE (LEFT TO RIGHT): Nasturtium leaves;
Basil; Mint; Lemon Balm; Dill.
BELOW (LEFT TO RIGHT): Lamb's lettuce;
Rocket; Flat-leaved Parsley; Sorrel; Lovage.*

in the salad bowl can always be cooked. Always choose young tender spinach leaves for salads.

To your lettuce basis, you will want to add other leaves. Watercress adds nearly year-round peppery savour; mustard and cress can be kept growing in its carton for 3-4 days if you remember to water it regularly; and in summer you may have nasturtium leaves from the garden for similar peppery purpose. Clusters of tender lamb's lettuce (mâche) and rocket are increasingly available from supermarkets, to add contrasts of flavour and texture.

Rocket seems to mark a growing supermarket overlap between salad leaves and herbs, and indeed you can increasingly find herbs, either in packets or potted and still growing, to add flavour and fragrance to your salads.

Like regular salad leaves, buy herbs as whole as you can, rinse and shake them and store low in the refrigerator loosely bagged in

polythene. Or, if they are in pots, keep them in the open, out of full sun, and remember to water them regularly. Large leaves of basil, essential to a proper tomato salad, are also good in a green salad. Whole leaves of flat-leaved parsley can go into the salad bowl. Mint is assertive and needs to be used with discretion, but lemon balm and sorrel are milder and can be added more liberally to leafy salads.

Dill is delicate and delicious with potatoes and broad beans as well as in salads featuring fish or eggs. For sturdier bean salads, the strong celery flavour of lovage makes a vigorous addition.

SALAD DRESSINGS

It's always best to dress a green salad at the very last minute, though salads of beans or other cooked vegetables usually benefit from a longer soak in their dressing.

Your oil base may be all olive oil, or olive mixed with a small

proportion of nut oil. Red wine vinegar is most popular, with sherry vinegar rather more refined, and balsamic vinegar the most luxurious of the lot. Often a splash of balsamic or raspberry vinegar is all that's needed in conjunction with sherry or wine vinegar.

You may choose to season either the salad or the dressing, but flavouring ingredients, such as mustard and garlic, should be added to the dressing. Sweetening is not usually desirable for leafy salads, but honey can be an improvement for winter salads of grated roots, particularly in a dressing mixed with cider vinegar and grainy mustard.

The basic formula for a vinaigrette is at least four and up to six parts of oil to one of vinegar or lemon juice. Start out with that and fine tune according to taste. It's easier to shake than stir, so mix your dressing in a screw-topped jar and shake it up to re-emulsify immediately before you toss it into the salad.

CHILLED BEETROOT AND APPLE SOUP

A cool, deep crimson soup that's as wonderfully refreshing to eat as it looks. Serve it topped with a dollop of minted cucumber cream – to mix in at the table. Grissini bread sticks are an ideal accompaniment.

SERVES 4

350 g (12 oz) cooked, peeled beetroot
juice of ½ lemon
600 ml (1 pint) unsweetened apple juice, chilled
200 g (7 oz) Greek-style yogurt, chilled
salt and pepper
cayenne pepper
10 cm (4 inch) piece cucumber
6 fresh mint leaves
6-8 fresh chives
TO SERVE
chives and mint sprigs, to garnish
grissini bread sticks

PREPARATION TIME
10 minutes
COOKING TIME
Nil
FREEZING
Not suitable

160 CALS PER SERVING

1. Slice the beetroot and place in a food processor or blender. Add the lemon juice, half the apple juice and half the yogurt. Process for 1-2 minutes until smooth.

2. Pour the beetroot mixture into a mixing bowl, stir in the rest of the apple juice and season with salt, pepper and cayenne pepper to taste. Chill until you are ready to serve, then pour into individual soup bowls.

3. To make the cucumber cream, grate the cucumber and stir into the remaining yogurt. Chop the mint and stir into the mixture. Spoon some cucumber cream into the middle of each serving and sprinkle with a little cayenne pepper. Snip some chives over the top and garnish with mint. Serve at once, accompanied by the bread sticks.

NOTE: If there is time, pass the puréed beetroot through a sieve to yield a smoother soup.

VARIATION

For the cucumber cream, use crème fraîche instead of Greek-style yogurt.

TECHNIQUE

For the cucumber cream, grate the cucumber into the yogurt.

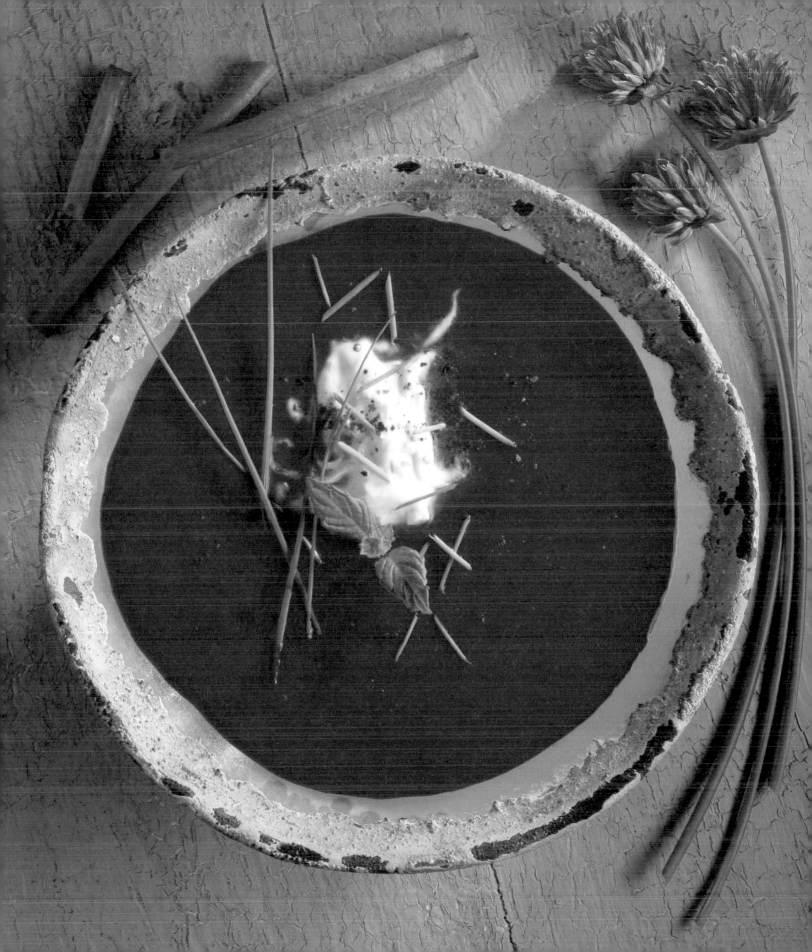

LEEK AND POTATO SOUP

A most satisfying soup that requires no stock. The method is derived from the Portuguese formula for cabbage soup, in which potato and garlic are mashed into their cooking water and the greenery added to cook down. Use the best olive oil you can muster for the vital finishing splash of flavour.

SERVES 4

575 g (1¼ lb) floury
   potatoes
2-3 garlic cloves
salt and pepper
350 g (12 oz) trimmed leeks
celery salt (optional)
60 ml (4 tbsp) coarsely
   chopped fresh parsley
60 ml (4 tbsp) extra-virgin
   olive oil
TO SERVE
sun-dried tomato bread

PREPARATION TIME
10 minutes
COOKING TIME
15 minutes
FREEZING
Not suitable

260 CALS PER SERVING

1. Peel and thinly slice the potatoes and garlic. Place in a saucepan and add 1.2 litres (2 pints) cold water. Bring to the boil and add salt. Cover and simmer for about 10 minutes until the potatoes are soft.

2. Meanwhile, slice the leeks. Add them to the potatoes and simmer for a further 5 minutes or so to soften the leeks.

3. Roughly mash the potatoes into the soup, using a potato masher. Correct the seasoning with celery salt (if available) and pepper to taste. Stir in the chopped parsley.

4. Ladle the soup into warmed soup plates and dribble 15 ml (1 tbsp) olive oil in a Z-slash over the surface of each serving. Serve immediately, with chunks of sun-dried tomato bread.

NOTE: Never be tempted to use a food processor or blender to mash potatoes, as it will make the texture gluey.

VARIATION

Use coarsely chopped watercress instead of parsley.

TECHNIQUE

Roughly mash the potatoes in the soup to thicken the liquor.

FATTOUSH

A glorious flavourful Arabic salad that's reminiscent of a rather solid Gazpacho. It's good eaten on its own as a starter or light lunch. Alternatively, it can be topped with a fried egg and served as a supper dish.

SERVES 4

4 tomatoes
½ cucumber
4 spring onions
1 small green pepper
1 garlic clove, crushed
juice of ½ lemon
30 ml (2 tbsp) finely
   chopped fresh parsley
45 ml (3 tbsp) olive oil
salt and pepper
1 pitta bread
TO GARNISH
roughly torn mint leaves
black olives

PREPARATION TIME
15 minutes
COOKING TIME
2-3 minutes
FREEZING
Not suitable

185 CALS PER SERVING

1. Preheat the grill. Put the tomatoes into a heatproof bowl and pour on boiling water to cover. Leave for 1 minute, then drain and remove the skins. Cut them up roughly and place in a food processor or blender. Cut the cucumber roughly and place in the food processor too.

2. Trim and roughly chop the spring onions. Halve, core and deseed the green pepper, then roughly chop the flesh. Add the spring onions and green pepper to the food processor with the garlic and lemon juice. Process to a chunky purée.

3. Turn the mixture into a bowl and stir in the chopped parsley, olive oil, salt and pepper.

4. Toast the pitta bread briefly on both sides. Break into small pieces and scatter over the salad.

5. Transfer the salad to a serving dish. Tear the mint leaves over the salad and stud with black olives.

NOTE: You can make this salad by hand if you prefer – chopping all the vegetables finely – but it will take a little longer.

TECHNIQUE

Break up the toasted pitta bread into small pieces and scatter over the salad.

LOCKETS SAVOURY

This recipe dates back to the days when smart West End restaurants – including one called 'Lockets' – served a savoury as well as, or instead of, a dessert at the end of a meal. This is a particularly luscious one, too good to fall into oblivion. Serve it instead as a starter.

SERVES 4

8 thick slices cut from a large baguette
1 packet ready-washed watercress (see note)
2 large ripe pears
225 g (8 oz) blue Stilton cheese
freshly ground black pepper

PREPARATION TIME
10 minutes
COOKING TIME
6-7 minutes
FREEZING
Not suitable

350 CALS PER SERVING

1. Preheat the grill and toast the bread on both sides. Trim the watercress sprigs. Peel, core and slice the pears.

2. Leaving the grill on, transfer the slices of toasted bread to a baking sheet that will hold them in a close single layer.

3. Cover with the watercress and place the pear slices on top. Slice the cheese and arrange over the pears.

4. Place under the grill until the cheese is just beginning to melt. Grind black pepper liberally over the top and serve at once.

NOTE: If you buy your watercress in bunches, allow a few extra minutes preparation time for washing, thorough drying and picking over.

VARIATION

Substitute another blue cheese, such as Gorgonzola or Bleu d'Auvergne.

TECHNIQUE

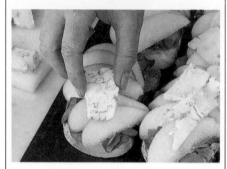

Slice the cheese and arrange over the pear slices.

FRENCH BEAN AND OMELETTE RIBBON SALAD

Thin strips of omelette festoon slim French beans in this pretty salad, which is enhanced by a vigorous dressing – full of Mediterranean flavours. Serve accompanied by olive bread.

SERVES 4

2 eggs
salt and pepper
50 ml (2 fl oz) olive oil
350 g (12 oz) French beans
1 large garlic clove
5 ml (1 tsp) red wine vinegar
5 ml (1 tsp) balsamic
  vinegar
2 sun-dried tomatoes, in oil,
  drained
5 ml (1 tsp) capers

PREPARATION TIME
15 minutes
COOKING TIME
8-9 minutes
FREEZING
Not suitable

210 CALS PER SERVING

1. Break the eggs into a bowl, season with salt and pepper and beat lightly with a fork. Smear an 18-20 cm (7-8 inch) frying pan (preferably non-stick) with a little olive oil and place over a moderate heat. When it is hot, pour in half the egg mixture and swirl the pan to spread the mixture quickly. It will set almost immediately into a thin omelette. Turn out onto a plate and repeat with the remaining egg, turning it out onto a separate plate.

2. Top and tail the French beans and cook them in a little boiling salted water for about 5 minutes. Drain and spread in a serving dish.

3. Peel the garlic and slice very thinly. Heat 15 ml (1 tbsp) olive oil in a pan, add the garlic and fry very briefly until it sizzles. Immediately add the remaining olive oil and vinegars to arrest cooking, and swirl vigorously together.

4. Chop the sun-dried tomatoes; chop the capers coarsely. Swirl them into the dressing and season with pepper, adding a little salt only if needed. Pour the dressing over the salad.

5. Slice the omelettes into 5 mm (¼ inch) ribbons and curl them loosely over the beans. Serve the salad accompanied by olive bread.

NOTE: The garlic should not brown or it will turn bitter.

VARIATION

Use runner beans when they are in season; you will need 450 g (1 lb). String the beans and slice diagonally, allowing 8-10 minutes' extra preparation time.

TECHNIQUE

Pour half of the egg mixture into the frying pan and swirl around the pan to spread evenly and make a thin omelette.

EGGS WITH SMOKED SALMON AND BLACK PEPPER

A sumptuous starter that's made in the time it takes to boil an egg! It's best if the soured cream is at room temperature when you use it, and if the eggs are still just warm when you serve them.

SERVES 4

4 eggs
50 g (2 oz) smoked salmon
150 ml (¼ pint) soured
    cream
5 ml (1 tsp) black
    peppercorns
TO SERVE
snipped chives or mustard
    and cress, to garnish
hot wholemeal toast,
    buttered

PREPARATION TIME
5 minutes
COOKING TIME
3½-5 minutes
FREEZING
Not suitable

190 CALS PER SERVING

1. Lower the eggs into a pan of simmering water, making sure that the water covers them completely. Cook for 3½-5 minutes until soft-boiled according to taste. Drain and rinse under cold running water until they are cool enough to handle, then shell them.

2. While the eggs are cooking, chop the smoked salmon roughly and mix into the soured cream. Crack the black peppercorns, using a pestle and mortar.

3. Halve the eggs and arrange on individual serving plates. Trickle the smoked salmon sauce over them. Scatter on the cracked black peppercorns and garnish with chives or mustard and cress. Serve at once with hot buttered toast.

NOTE: If you haven't got a pestle and mortar, then grind the peppercorns as coarsely as you can over the dish.

EGGS: 'At risk' groups including the elderly, pregnant women, babies, young children and people who have immune-deficiency disease are advised to avoid eating lightly cooked (or raw) eggs, due to the possible risk of salmonella.

VARIATION

For a more sophisticated starter, replace the hen's eggs with 12 quail eggs. Bring them to the boil, cook for 1 minute, then drain and shell. Finish as above.

TECHNIQUE

Crack the black peppercorns using a pestle and mortar, to release their flavour.

CALABRIAN PASTA

The finest broccoli is grown right down in the toe of Italy, in Calabria – and called calabrese after the region. Fried with pine nuts, sultanas, garlic and breadcrumbs, it makes a delicious sauce to serve with the local pasta, ziti – which resembles spaghetti-length macaroni. You can, of course, use spaghetti or long fusilli instead.

SERVES 4-6

150 g (5 oz) broccoli
50 g (2 oz) sultanas
300-350 g (10-12 oz) ziti,
    long fusilli or spaghetti
salt and pepper
2 garlic cloves
125 ml (4 fl oz) olive oil
75 g (3 oz) white
    breadcrumbs
25 g (1 oz) pine nuts
10 ml (2 tsp) anchovy
    essence or anchovy paste
45 ml (3 tbsp) chopped fresh
    parsley
cayenne pepper, to taste

PREPARATION TIME
10 minutes
COOKING TIME
12-15 minutes
FREEZING
Fresh breadcrumbs can be
frozen and fried straight from
the freezer

695-465 CALS PER SERVING

1. Bring about 600 ml (1 pint) water to the boil. Meanwhile, break the broccoli into small florets, cutting the stems into pieces about the same size; place in a saucepan. Put the sultanas in a bowl, pour on a little of the boiling water and leave to soak. Pour the rest of the boiling water over the broccoli, bring to the boil and simmer for 30 seconds; drain.

2. Cook the pasta in a large pan of boiling salted water until 'al dente', tender but firm to the bite.

3. In the meantime, peel and finely chop the garlic. Heat the oil in a frying pan and add the breadcrumbs. Fry, stirring until they begin to crisp, then add the garlic and pine nuts. Continue to fry, stirring, until the pine nuts begin to colour, then add the broccoli. Stir over the heat until the broccoli is thoroughly hot.

4. Drain the pasta in a colander, setting it back on top of the saucepan to catch the last 15 ml (1 tbsp) cooking water. Stir the anchovy essence or paste and drained sultanas into this liquid, then return the pasta to the pan. Toss with a generous grinding of black pepper and half of the chopped parsley. Transfer to a heated serving bowl.

5. Mix the remaining parsley into the crumb mixture and sprinkle over the pasta. Sprinkle with cayenne pepper and toss at the table.

NOTE: It's an Italian trick to toss the pasta with a little of its cooking water. This helps to keep the pasta hot, as well as preventing it from drying out.

TECHNIQUE

Fry the breadcrumbs with the garlic until golden and beginning to crisp, before adding the pine nuts.

STIR-FRIED KING PRAWNS ON SESAME NOODLES

Flavours are kept separate in this light, fast and sophisticated shellfish dish. Ginger and spring onions give piquancy to the prawns, soy and sesame add deep flavour to the noodles and vegetables. It's important that the prawns are raw, but you can buy them in various stages (see note). If you serve them with the shells on – which is the prettiest way – finger bowls on the table would be considerable.

SERVES 4

16 raw king prawns (see note)
150 g (5 oz) mangetouts
4 spring onions
7.5 cm (3 inch) piece fresh root ginger
10 ml (2 tsp) sesame seeds
5 ml (1 tsp) salt
250 g (9 oz) egg noodles
30 ml (2 tbsp) vegetable oil
juice of 1 lime
10 ml (2 tsp) shredded fresh coriander leaves
30 ml (2 tbsp) soy sauce
5 ml (1 tsp) sesame oil
TO SERVE
coriander leaves, to garnish
lime wedges
prawn crackers (optional)

PREPARATION TIME
10 minutes
COOKING TIME
10 minutes
FREEZING
Not suitable

410 CALS PER SERVING

1. If the prawns are frozen, thaw them in advance; if you buy them fresh, keep them refrigerated until you are ready to cook.

2. Top and tail the mangetouts. Trim and roughly chop the spring onions. Peel and grate the ginger. Put the sesame seeds in a small, heavy-based pan and shake over a medium heat until they begin to turn golden and develop a toasted aroma. Tip the toasted sesame seeds out on to a saucer.

3. Bring a large pan of water to the boil, add the salt and mangetouts and return to the boil. Simmer for 30 seconds, then drop in the egg noodles, turn off the heat and leave to stand for 6 minutes.

4. Meanwhile, heat the oil in a wide frying pan. Add the prawns and cook for 1½-2 minutes each side, scattering on the spring onions and ginger before you turn them. Squeeze on the lime juice and sprinkle on the coriander when the prawns are cooked.

5. Drain the noodles and mangetouts and toss in the soy sauce, sesame oil and toasted sesame seeds. Transfer to a heated serving dish or individual plates. Arrange the prawns and spring onions

on top and garnish with lime wedges. Serve immediately, with prawn crackers if desired.

NOTE: Raw king prawns are available fresh and frozen from good fishmongers and larger supermarket. Buy fresh ones in-shell and head-on, if possible. They are also sold shelled and headless, and in-shell but with heads removed.

VARIATION

Replace the coriander leaves with flat-leaved parsley.

TECHNIQUE

Add the ginger and spring onions to the prawns, then turn them to cook the other side.

TROUT WITH DILL AND HORSERADISH MAYONNAISE

Each pink-fleshed trout lies on a long leaf of Cos lettuce, making a simple, elegant dish – perfect for a supper party. The cooking is beautifully simple too, for the fish complete their cooking in the cooling poaching liquor. Serve with a potato salad, ideally in a hazelnut oil dressing and finished with a scattering of nuts.

SERVES 4

4 gutted trout, each about
    200 g (7 oz)
100 ml (3½ fl oz) white wine
    vinegar
10 ml (2 tsp) black
    peppercorns
10 ml (2 tsp) dill seeds
    (optional)
3 bay leaves
5 ml (1 tsp) salt
MAYONNAISE
1 Bramley apple, about
    150 g (5 oz)
150 ml (¼ pint) good-quality
    mayonnaise
45 ml (3 tbsp) chopped fresh
    dill leaves
10 ml (2 tsp) grated
    horseradish or
    horseradish sauce
TO SERVE
8 long Cos lettuce leaves
dill sprigs, bay leaves and
    lime wedges, to garnish

PREPARATION TIME
15 minutes
COOKING TIME
35-40 minutes, including cooling
FREEZING
Not suitable

560 CALS PER SERVING

1. Wash the fish inside and out under cold running water. Fill a large roasting tin with boiling water. Add the wine vinegar, peppercorns, dill seeds if using, bay leaves and salt. Immerse the fish in the liquid and bring back to the boil. As soon as it reaches the boil, turn off the heat and leave the fish undisturbed in the liquid for at least 20 minutes.

2. For the mayonnaise, peel, quarter, core and slice the apple. Place in a small pan with 45 ml (3 tbsp) water. Cover and cook until the apple is softened to a purée. Beat until smooth and allow to cool, then mix with the mayonnaise, chopped dill and horseradish.

3. Lift the trout from the poaching liquor, remove the skin, and their heads if preferred. Lay each fish in a long lettuce leaf on a serving plate and spoon some of the dill and apple mayonnaise alongside. Garnish with dill sprigs, bay leaves and lime wedges.

NOTE: Trout are often sold ready-gutted, but if they are whole allow a little extra weight and ask the fishmonger to gut them for you.

VARIATION

Use the same poaching method for a whole salmon, bringing to the boil then leaving to cool in the liquor, but put the salmon into *cold* seasoned water and raise the liquid to boiling point slowly.

TECHNIQUE

Carefully remove the skin from each trout to reveal the pink flesh.

OATMEAL AND DILL CRUSTED HERRINGS

It's an old Scottish habit to crust herrings with oatmeal, both to soak up the oils that exude from this nutritious fish and to provide contrast of texture. Here lemon zest and dill seed add extra zing. Lettuce wilts as it is heated with cucumber in butter and lemon juice provides sauce for the dish.

SERVES 4

4 herrings, each about 225 g
   (8 oz)
15 ml (1 tbsp) olive oil
45-60 ml (3-4 tbsp) pinhead
   oatmeal
5 ml (1 tsp) dill seed
finely grated rind and juice
   of 1 lemon
salt and pepper
½ cucumber
1 Little Gem lettuce
50 g (2 oz) butter
30 ml (2 tbsp) finely
   chopped fresh dill leaves
dill sprigs, to garnish

PREPARATION TIME
10 minutes
COOKING TIME
5-6 minutes
FREEZING
Not suitable

700 CALS PER SERVING

1. Ask the fishmonger to gut and fillet the herring, removing the heads. Rinse and pat dry with kitchen paper, then smear the fleshy surface of each fillet with olive oil. Preheat the grill. Line the grill rack with foil and arrange the fish flesh-side up on it.

2. Mix the oatmeal with the dill seed, grated lemon rind, and salt and pepper, then sprinkle the mixture evenly over the herring fillets. Pat down lightly to give a good coating.

3. Peel the cucumber, halve it lengthways and scoop out the seeds with a teaspoon. Cut each cucumber half crosswise into 1 cm (½ inch) slices. Cut the lettuce crosswise into slices of about the same thickness.

4. Grill the herrings, coated side up, for 4-5 minutes.

5. Meanwhile, melt the butter in a frying pan and add the lemon juice. Add the cucumber and lettuce and cook, stirring, until the lettuce wilts. Add the chopped dill and season with salt and pepper.

6. Transfer the grilled herrings to warmed serving plates and spoon the wilted lettuce and cucumber alongside. Garnish with dill to serve.

VARIATION

Use mackerel instead of herring fillets.

TECHNIQUE

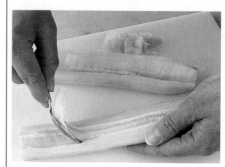

Scoop the seeds out of the peeled and halved cucumber, using a teaspoon.

UPPER-CRUST SEARED SALMON ON SPICED LENTILS

This fashionable method of cooking salmon on one side only crisps the skin while leaving the interior of the fish moist and rare. The top is barely cooked, but inverting the fillets on to a dish of hot Puy lentils completes the cooking process. Make sure the salmon fillets are at room temperature when you cook them.

SERVES 4

4 salmon fillets, each about
    125 g (4 oz), with skin
225 g (8 oz) Puy or brown
    lentils
2 bay leaves
1 small onion
1 celery stick, plus 4-5 celery
    leaves
salt and pepper
45 ml (3 tbsp) olive oil
10 ml (2 tsp) cumin seeds
juice of ½ lemon
TO SERVE
herb sprigs, to garnish
lemon wedges

PREPARATION TIME
10 minutes
COOKING TIME
20-25 minutes
FREEZING
Not suitable

505 CALS PER SERVING

1. Rinse the salmon fillets and pat dry with kitchen paper.

2. Wash the lentils thoroughly in a sieve under cold running water. Add to a pan of cold water and bring to the boil. Skim the surface, then add the bay leaves and simmer for 20-25 minutes, until just soft.

3. Meanwhile, peel and chop the onion. Remove any strings from the celery stick and chop finely. Shred the celery leaves and keep separate.

4. Rub salt into the skin of the salmon and grind black pepper on top. Smear a heavy-based frying pan with a little olive oil and place over a low heat. Place the fillets skin-side down in the pan and cook on this side only until the lower three quarters of the salmon is cooked. Do not turn the fish. Cooking time will vary according to thickness: allow 10 minutes for thin tail-end pieces; 2-3 minutes longer for thicker centre-cut fillets. The very top of the salmon should still appear undercooked (see note).

5. Meanwhile, put the cumin seeds in a separate frying pan over a medium heat, shaking the pan until they release their fragrance. Immediately add the remaining olive oil, the onion and celery. Cook, stirring frequently, for 6-7 minutes.

6. Drain the lentils and toss in the fried vegetables. Add the lemon juice, season generously with salt and pepper and stir the celery leaves through the lentils.

7. Spread the lentils on warmed serving plates and immediately lay the salmon fillets upside down on top of them. Garnish with herbs and serve with lemon wedges.

NOTE: It is most important that the lentils are very hot to complete the cooking of the fish. If they are ready ahead of time, stir them into the fried vegetables and reheat immediately before serving.

TECHNIQUE

Cook the salmon fillets, skin-side down, until the lower three quarters of each one is cooked. Quickly remove from the pan and invert onto the lentils to complete the cooking.

MADRAS HADDOCK FILLETS WITH RICE AND PEAS

Arichly spiced marinade combines with a dredging of flour to give tender fish fillets a delicious crisp golden coating. The haddock fillets are served on a bed of buttery rice and peas, flavoured with cumin seeds.

4 skinned haddock fillets,
    each about 125 g (4 oz)
½ onion
5 cm (2 inch) piece fresh
    root ginger
I egg
5 ml (I tsp) turmeric
5 ml (I tsp) ground coriander
2.5 ml (½ tsp) chilli powder
salt and pepper
juice of ½ lemon
plain white flour, for coating
oil, for shallow-frying
RICE
½ onion
50 g (2 oz) butter
10 ml (2 tsp) cumin seeds
200 g (7 oz) long-grain white
    rice
juice of ½ lemon
125 g (4 oz) frozen peas
30 ml (2 tbsp) chopped fresh
    coriander or parsley
TO GARNISH
lemon wedges

PREPARATION TIME
10 minutes
COOKING TIME
25 minutes
FREEZING
Not suitable

550 CALS PER SERVING

I. First prepare the rice. Peel and chop the half-onion. Melt the butter in a saucepan, add the onion and cumin seeds and cook, stirring, until the onion is softened.

2. Add the rice and stir until it is thoroughly coated in the butter. Add the lemon juice, 450 ml (¾ pint) water and 5 ml (I tsp) salt, and bring to the boil. Stir in the peas, cover, turn the heat down as low as possible and cook for 12 minutes. Turn off the heat without uncovering the pan and leave for a further 10 minutes or so.

3. Meanwhile, lay the haddock fillets on a glass (or china) plate. Grate the half-onion, or mince it in a food processor. Peel and grate the ginger. Break the egg into a bowl and add the onion, ginger, spices, salt, pepper and lemon juice. Pour over the fish, turning to coat the fillets with the marinade and leave until the rice is almost ready.

4. Dredge the haddock fillets in flour to coat quite thickly, forming a batter with the marinade. Heat a I cm (½ inch) depth of oil in a frying pan and fry the fish for 2-3 minutes on each side. Drain the fish on kitchen paper and keep hot.

5. Meanwhile, grind black pepper over the rice, scatter on the coriander or parsley, then fork up lightly. Divide between warmed serving plates and top with the fish fillets. Garnish with lemon wedges and serve at once.

NOTE: If you have more time, prepare the fish marinade first and allow the fish to marinate for up to I hour.

VARIATION

Use any other firm-fleshed white fish fillets – such as cod or hoki – in place of the haddock.

TECHNIQUE

Dredge the spiced fish fillets with flour to coat quite thickly and form a batter with the marinade.

NORMANDY SKATE WITH CAPER SAUCE

A sweet flavour and lack of bones make skate an appealing fish, and it is available most of the year round. However, it is imperative to avoid overcooking it, otherwise the central cartilaginous framework will begin to break down, spoiling both texture and flavour.

SERVES 4

4 piece of skate wing, each
  about 200 g (7 oz)
2 shallots
1 celery stick
2 bay leaves
5 ml (1 tsp) black
  peppercorns
75 ml (5 tbsp) cider vinegar
10 ml (2 tsp) capers
150 ml (¼ pint) double
  cream
30 ml (2 tbsp) chopped fresh
  parsley
salt and pepper
parsley sprigs, to garnish

PREPARATION TIME
5 minutes
COOKING TIME
15-20 minutes
FREEZING
Not suitable

330 CALS PER SERVING

1. Ask your fishmonger to skin the skate wings if necessary, and cut to the right portion size.

2. Peel and roughly chop the shallots. Break the celery stick into 3 or 4 pieces. Put these into a large saucepan with the bay leaves, black peppercorns and 60 ml (4 tbsp) of the cider vinegar. Add 1.2 litres (2 pints) cold water, slide in the skate and slowly bring to just below the boil — the surface should barely bubble.

3. Cover the pan, lower the heat and cook for 7-10 minutes, until the skate flesh just parts from the central cartilaginous layer.

4. While the fish is cooking, chop the capers and put them into a small pan with the cream. Stir in the parsley and season with salt and pepper. Bring to the boil, lower the heat and simmer for 1 minute. Take off the heat and stir in the remaining 15 ml (1 tbsp) vinegar. Check the seasoning.

5. Lift the skate from the poaching liquor on to warmed serving plates. Spoon on the cream sauce and garnish with parsley sprigs. Serve immediately, accompanied by boiled new potatoes and a green vegetable.

NOTE: Drain the skate scrupulously as you lift it from the poaching liquor and flick off any flavouring debris adhering to the fish.

TECHNIQUE

Slide the skate wings into the cold poaching liquor, then slowly bring to the boil.

COD CUTLETS PROVENÇALE

Robust flavours and bright colour contrasts characterise this southern treatment of fish from northern waters. Scarlet tomatoes, shiny black olives and vivid green basil leaves offset the white fish perfectly, and a splash of aniseed liqueur gives the dish resonant depth.

SERVES 4

4 cod cutlets, each about
   150 g (5 oz)
1 Spanish onion
75 ml (5 tbsp) olive oil
5 ml (1 tsp) dried oregano
3 garlic cloves
400 g (14 oz) can peeled
   plum tomatoes
15 ml (1 tbsp) tomato purée
10 ml (2 tsp) pastis, ouzo or
   other aniseed liqueur
salt and pepper
12 small black olives
1-2 fresh basil sprigs
extra basil sprigs, to garnish

PREPARATION TIME
10 minutes
COOKING TIME
About 25 minutes
FREEZING
Not suitable

325 CALS PER SERVING

1. Rinse the fish cutlets and pat dry with kitchen paper; set aside.

2. Peel and chop the onion very finely. Heat the olive oil in a large shallow frying pan. Add the onion with the oregano and cook over a very low heat for 10 minutes, stirring frequently. Meanwhile, peel and finely chop or crush the garlic; add to the pan and cook for a further 2-3 minutes until the onion is translucent and beginning to turn pale golden.

3. Add the tomatoes to the pan, mashing with a fork to break them down. Add the tomato purée, bring to the boil and stir in the liqueur. Season with salt and pepper to taste.

4. Bury the fish cutlets in the tomato sauce and scatter the olives between them. Cover and cook gently for 6 minutes, then turn the fish cutlets over and continue cooking for a further 4-5 minutes, until you can just pull the flesh from the bone with the tip of a knife.

5. Check the seasoning of the sauce. Tear the basil leaves over the dish and serve immediately, garnished with extra basil sprigs.

NOTE: Ricard is the best-known brand of pastis. Pernod is similarly flavoured with anise and has the same effect in cooking.

VARIATIONS

Use other white fish steaks – such as swordfish or haddock. If you have no aniseed-flavoured liqueur, fry a teaspoonful of fennel seeds with the onion.

TECHNIQUE

Add the fish cutlets to the pan, burying them in the sauce.

GRILLED STEAKS WITH SHALLOTS AND WINE

An old-fashioned French classic for hurried cooks in search of a treat. Croûtes of French bread are used to mop up the delicious juices from the grill pan and served on the side. A green salad and a bottle of good red wine from Bordeaux are the only other accompaniments you'll need.

SERVES 4

225 g (8 oz) shallots
50 g (2 oz) chilled butter
350 ml (12 fl oz) red
   Bordeaux wine
4 sirloin steaks, each about
   175-200 g (6-7 oz)
30 ml (2 tbsp) vegetable oil
8 slices French bread
10-15 ml (2-3 tsp) Dijon
   mustard
30 ml (2 tbsp) chopped fresh
   parsley
parsley sprigs, to garnish

PREPARATION TIME
15 minutes while grill preheats
COOKING TIME
4-12 minutes
FREEZING
Not suitable

555 CALS PER SERVING

1. Preheat the grill. Peel and chop the shallots. Melt 15 g (½ oz) of the butter in a saucepan. Add the shallots and sauté for a few minutes until slightly softened. Add the wine and bring to the boil. Simmer, uncovered, until the wine is reduced by half and the shallots are soft.

2. Smear the steaks on both sides with the oil and arrange on the grill rack. Cook, as close to the heat as possible, turning the steaks every 2 minutes. Allow 4 minutes (one turn) for very rare steaks; 8 minutes (three turns) for medium. For well-done steaks allow 12 minutes, increasing the time between turns to 3 minutes. Season the steaks with salt and pepper as you make the final turn.

3. Meanwhile, cut the remaining butter into 6 cubes and beat one at a time into the shallot sauce, making sure each one is totally absorbed before adding the next.

4. Transfer the steaks to warmed serving plates and keep warm. Press the bread slices onto the grill pan to soak up the juices, then spread each lightly with Dijon mustard. Put 2 slices beside each steak. Pour the sauce over the steaks, sprinkle with chopped parsley and serve garnished with sprigs of parsley.

NOTE: The technique of beating cold diced butter into a hot wine-based sauce is called 'mounting'. It thickens the sauce slightly and gives a glossy finish.

VARIATIONS

Use rump rather than sirloin steaks. Use a hot griddle pan to cook the steaks, rather than grill them.

TECHNIQUE

After cooking the steaks, rub the slices of French bread around the grill pan to gather up the pan juices.

SPICED LAMB WITH SPINACH AND POTATO

Lean and tender lamb leg steaks cook quickly under the grill. Here they are finished with a creamy topping that bathes the meat in spices as it melts to a rich golden sauce. Spicy vegetables are the perfect complement.

SERVES 4

4 boneless leg steaks of
    lamb, each about 150-175 g
    (5-6 oz)
juice of 1 lemon
3 garlic cloves, crushed
15 ml (1 tbsp) chilli oil (see
    note)
1 onion
575 g (1¼ lb) small new
    potatoes
10 ml (2 tsp) mustard seeds
60 ml (4 tbsp) vegetable oil
300 g (10 oz) packet frozen
    leaf spinach
salt and pepper
5 ml (1 tsp) ground cumin
5 cm (2 inch) piece fresh
    root ginger
7.5 ml (1½ tsp) turmeric
60 ml (4 tbsp) crème fraîche
    or Greek yogurt
few mint leaves, shredded
cayenne pepper, to taste
mint sprigs, to garnish

PREPARATION TIME
15 minutes
COOKING TIME
25 minutes
FREEZING
Not suitable

545 CALS PER SERVING

1. Lay the lamb steaks in a shallow dish and sprinkle with half of the lemon juice. Spread half of the garlic over the meat, then sprinkle a few drops of chilli oil onto both sides of each steak. Rub the garlic, oil and lemon juice well into the meat.

2. Peel and chop the onion. Wash the potatoes and halve any larger ones. Preheat the grill.

3. Put the mustard seeds in a dry heavy-based pan over a medium heat, cover and shake the pan until the popping dies down. Add 45 ml (3 tbsp) of the oil and the chopped onion. Cook, stirring frequently, over a low heat for 5 minutes. Add the potatoes and remaining garlic. Cook for a further 2 minutes.

4. Add the spinach, remaining lemon juice and 5 ml (1 tsp) each of salt and ground cumin. Stir until the spinach thaws, then cover and leave to cook for 15 minutes.

5. Meanwhile, peel and grate the ginger and mix with the turmeric and remaining 15 ml (1 tbsp) oil. Stir in the crème fraîche or yogurt. Season with salt and pepper.

6. Line the rack of the grill pan with foil, lay the lamb steaks on top and grill for 5 minutes on one side. Turn and spread the cream or yogurt mixture over the uncooked side of the meat and return to the grill for 5 minutes.

7. Uncover the vegetables towards the end of the cooking time if there is too much liquid, to allow the excess to evaporate. Just before serving, add the shredded mint, black pepper, and more salt if necessary.

8. Divide the vegetables between warmed serving plates and place the lamb steaks alongside. Sprinkle a little cayenne over each one. Garnish with extra mint sprigs to serve.

NOTE: If you haven't any chilli-flavoured oil, use ordinary vegetable oil adding a dash of Tabasco.

TECHNIQUE

Spread the spiced yogurt over the turned leg steaks.

KOFTAS ON GREEN HERBS WITH TOMATO RICE

For this North African dish, spiced minced meat – usually lamb, but sometimes beef or a mixture of both – is packed cylindrically around skewers, then grilled to a crust. The koftas are served on a bed of herbs and spring onions, and accompanied by tasty tomato-flavoured rice.

SERVES 4

575 g (1¼ lb) finely minced lamb
1 onion
5 ml (1 tsp) ground allspice
6 fresh mint leaves, or 5 ml (1 tsp) dried mint
salt and pepper
olive oil, for brushing
TOMATO RICE
2 garlic cloves
30 ml (2 tbsp) olive oil
225 g (8 oz) long-grain rice
200 g (7 oz) can peeled plum tomatoes
TO SERVE
3 spring onions
45 ml (3 tbsp) chopped parsley
lemon wedges
parsley sprigs

PREPARATION TIME
20 minutes
COOKING TIME
About 25 minutes
FREEZING
Not suitable

590 CALS PER SERVING

1. First prepare the tomato rice. Peel and finely chop the garlic. Heat the oil in a heavy-based saucepan (which has a close-fitting lid). Add the garlic and fry gently for 1 minute. Add the rice and stir over the heat for 1 minute until is glossy.

2. Tip the can of tomatoes into a sieve over the saucepan and press through, then fill the can with cold water and pour that in too. Bring to the boil and season with salt and pepper. Cover with a tight-fitting lid, turn the heat down as low as possible and simmer for 10 minutes.

3. Line the grill rack with foil and pre-heat the grill. Put the minced lamb into a bowl. Peel the onion and grate it over the meat. Shred the fresh mint finely if using. Sprinkle the mint, allspice, salt and pepper over the lamb and use your hands to mix together thoroughly to a paste. Divide into 8 portions and mould each into a sausage shape around a skewer. Brush them all over with olive oil.

4. When the rice has simmered for 10 minutes, turn off heat without removing lid, and leave for a further 12-15 minutes.

5. In the meantime, arrange the meat skewers on the lined grill pan and grill, turning regularly, for about 10-12 minutes until well browned all over.

6. Meanwhile, trim and chop the spring onions, mix with the parsley and spread in a layer on one side of each serving plate. Lay the koftas on top.

7. Fork up the rice gently, correct the seasoning and serve with the koftas. Garnish with lemon wedges and parsley.

NOTE: If wooden skewers are used, soak them in cold water for at least 10 minutes before packing the meat around them. This prevents exposed tips from burning during grilling.

VARIATION

Use finely minced beef instead of lamb, or a mixture of both.

TECHNIQUE

Mould the meat paste around 8 skewers, to form sausage shapes, 12-15 cm (5-6 inches) long.

GARLIC AND HONEY PORK WITH VEGETABLE NOODLES

Lean, thin cuts of tender meat, pork tenderloins can be quickly cooked in a hot oven. The savoury liquid that flavours the meat during cooking then dresses the vegetables and noodles that accompany it.

SERVES 4

2 pork tenderloins (fillets),
   each about 250 g (9 oz)
5 cm (2 inch) piece fresh
   root ginger
3 garlic cloves, crushed
30 ml (2 tbsp) thin honey
45 ml (3 tbsp) soy sauce
45 ml (3 tbsp) dry sherry
15 ml (1 tbsp) vegetable oil
10 ml (2 tsp) sesame seeds
VEGETABLE NOODLES
1 large yellow pepper
4 spring onions
2 lemon grass stalks
225 g (8 oz) beansprouts
grated rind and juice of
   ½ lemon
15 ml (1 tbsp) sesame oil
125 g (4 oz) rice noodles
30 ml (2 tbsp) vegetable oil

PREPARATION TIME
20 minutes
COOKING TIME
25 minutes
FREEZING
Not suitable

490 CALS PER SERVING

1. Preheat the oven to 220°C (425°F) Mark 7. Trim any fat and membrane from the pork tenderloins and prick them all over with a fork. Arrange them side by side but not touching in a roasting tin.

2. Peel and grate the ginger. Mix the garlic, ginger, honey, soy sauce, sherry and oil together in a bowl, then pour over the pork tenderloins, turning them to coat all over.

3. Roast in the oven for 25 minutes, turning the pork, basting and sprinkling with the sesame seeds after 15 minutes.

4. Meanwhile, prepare the 'vegetable noodles'. Halve the pepper lengthways. Remove the core and seeds, then shred finely. Trim the spring onions and slice diagonally. Remove the coarse outer leaves from the lemon grass, then shred the stalks very thinly. Rinse and drain the beansprouts in a large colander. Mix the lemon rind and juice with the sesame oil.

5. When the meat is ready, leave to stand in the switched-off oven. Put the noodles in a heatproof bowl, pour on boiling water to cover and stir to separate the noodles.

6. Heat the oil in a wok or sauté pan, add the yellow pepper, spring onions

and lemon grass and stir-fry for 1 minute. Drain the noodles through the beansprouts in the colander, shake well and add to the stir-fry.

7. Transfer the pork tenderloins to a carving board. Pour the liquid from the roasting tin over the noodle mixture. Add the lemon and sesame oil mixture and stir-fry briefly. Carve the meat into slices, about 5 mm (¼ inch) thick, and serve with the vegetable noodles.

TECHNIQUE

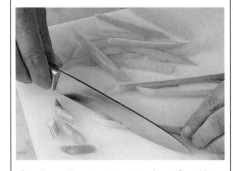

Cut the yellow pepper into long fine slices. Slice the spring onions on the diagonal.

SAUSAGE COILED IN A CAKE TIN

The sausage has risen to new heights of respectability recently, due to a proliferation of specialist shops making worthy bangers on the premises, and the supermarket response with new premium sausages. Serve your sausage proudly in a sauce chunky with vegetables – and if you are opening a bottle of wine to drink with it, as this dish certainly deserves, add a splash to the pan too.

SERVES 4

450 g (1 lb) Cumberland or
    other high-quality sausage
    (preferably unlinked)
12 shallots
30 ml (2 tbsp) vegetable oil
400 g (14 oz) can peeled
    plum tomatoes
5 ml (1 tsp) dried oregano
200 g (7 oz) frozen peas
10 ml (2 tsp)
    Worcestershire sauce
30 ml (2 tbsp) red wine
    (optional)
salt and pepper

PREPARATION TIME
20 minutes while oven preheats
COOKING TIME
25 minutes
FREEZING
Not suitable

540 CALS PER SERVING

1. Preheat the oven to 220°C (425°F) Mark 7. If the sausage you are using is twisted in links, untwist between each sausage and gently massage the meat towards the middle to form an even cylinder. Twist the skin at the ends and trim off surplus skin.

2. Peel the shallots; if large, cut in half. Oil a 20 cm (8 inch) shallow cake tin (with a solid base). Coil the sausage in the middle of the tin and arrange the shallots around the edge. Brush both sausage and shallots with more oil. Bake in the oven for about 25 minutes until the sausage is a deep brown colour and shiny on top.

3. Meanwhile, drain the tomatoes, tip them into a saucepan and mash roughly. Add the oregano, peas, Worcestershire sauce and red wine if using. Cook gently until the peas are tender. Season with salt and pepper.

4. Cut the cooked sausage into wedges. Transfer the sausage and shallots to warmed serving plates and spoon on the tomatoes and peas. Serve with mashed potatoes or hot French bread.

NOTE: Cumberland sausage is traditionally sold untwisted in a continuous coil. If your sausages are linked, you will first need to untwist them.

VARIATION

Vary the dish with any of the new flavours of sausage now available.

TECHNIQUE

Coil the sausage in a solid-based 20 cm (8 inch) shallow cake tin, arranging the shallots around the edge.

SOY DUCK BREASTS WITH PAPAYA SALSA

Barbary duck breasts are leaner and meatier than the more readily available 'Aylesbury' duck breasts, and can be fast-roasted. Serve with a fruity salsa of papaya spiked with chilli, and crisp green beans freckled with toasted sesame seeds.

SERVES 4

4 Barbary duck breast fillets,
    each about 175 g (6 oz)
    (see note)
5 cm (2 inch) piece fresh
    root ginger
finely grated rind and juice
    of 1 lime
30 ml (2 tbsp) soy sauce
10 ml (2 tsp) soft brown
    sugar
450 g (1 lb) runner beans, or
    350 g (12 oz) French
    beans
10 ml (2 tsp) sesame seeds
1 papaya
3 spring onions
1 red chilli
handful of fresh coriander
    leaves
salt
10 ml (2 tsp) sesame oil
TO GARNISH
coriander sprigs
lime wedges

PREPARATION TIME
20 minutes
COOKING TIME
About 20 minutes
FREEZING
Not suitable

480 CALS PER SERVING

1. Position a shelf near the top of the oven and preheat the oven to 230°C (450°F) Mark 8.

2. Make diagonal cuts through the fat of the duck breasts at 1 cm (½ inch) intervals. Grate the ginger and mix with the lime rind, soy sauce and sugar in a roasting tin. Put the duck breasts in the tin, fat-side down, then turn them fat-side up.

3. String the runner beans and cut into long slices on the diagonal, or simply top and tail French beans. Put the sesame seeds in a heavy-based pan and shake over a moderate heat until they begin to darken and develop a toasted aroma; turn out onto a saucer and set aside.

4. Put the duck breasts in their roasting tin on the high oven shelf. Roast for about 20 minutes, until the skin is crisp and well browned, and the flesh is tender.

5. Meanwhile, halve the papaya and scoop out the seeds. Remove the peel and dice the flesh; place in a serving bowl. Trim and finely chop the spring onions; halve, deseed and finely chop the chilli; add both to the papaya. Chop the coriander leaves and add to the salsa ingredients, with the lime juice. Mix together, seasoning with salt to taste.

6. Cook the beans in boiling salted water for 4-5 minutes, so they are still crisp. Drain, then toss in the sesame oil and toasted sesame seeds.

7. Carve the duck breasts into slices on the diagonal. Fan out on warmed serving plates, pouring a little of the pan juices over the duck. Garnish with coriander sprigs and lime wedges. Serve with the papaya salsa and green beans.

NOTE: For this fast-roasting the meat must be at room temperature when you start cooking. If you are only able to obtain the larger 350 g (12 oz) duck breasts, buy 2 rather than 4, and increase the cooking time to 25-30 minutes.

TECHNIQUE

Score through the skin and fat of the duck breasts on the diagonal, using a sharp knife. This encourages the fat to run out and the skin to crisp during cooking.

CHICKEN BREASTS WITH PAPRIKA MUSHROOM SAUCE

A rich, warmly spiced mushroom sauce adds excitement to quickly cooked chicken breast fillets. Serve with a green vegetable, such as baby leeks or mangetouts, and sauté potatoes flavoured with garlic.

SERVES 4

15 g (½ oz) dried porcini mushrooms (see note)

45 ml (3 tbsp) medium dry sherry, preferably Amontillado

1 small onion

200 g (7 oz) chestnut or cup mushrooms

30 ml (2 tbsp) vegetable oil

50 g (2 oz) butter

4 skinless chicken breast fillets

5 ml (1 tsp) chopped fresh or dried thyme

125 ml (4 fl oz) crème fraîche

about 125 ml (4 fl oz) chicken stock

15 ml (1 tbsp) paprika

salt and pepper

PREPARATION TIME
10 minutes
COOKING TIME
20-25 minutes
FREEZING
Not suitable

480 CALS PER SERVING

1. Put the porcini mushrooms in a small bowl. Warm the sherry, pour over the porcini and leave to stand. Peel the onion and chop finely. Slice the fresh mushrooms.

2. Heat the oil and 25 g (1 oz) of the butter in a frying pan. Add the chicken breasts and cook for about 5 minutes each side. Lift out the chicken with a slotted spoon and transfer to a warmed dish; cover and keep warm.

3. Add the onion and thyme to the pan and fry over a gentle heat, stirring frequently, for 5 minutes. Add the remaining butter, then add the fresh mushrooms and cook, stirring, over a moderate heat for 5 minutes.

4. Add the porcini with their soaking liquid and cook for 1 minute, then add the crème fraîche. Stir in sufficient stock to thin the sauce to the desired consistency, and add the paprika. Cook for 2 minutes, then check the seasoning. Pour the sauce over the chicken breasts to serve.

NOTE: If porcini or other dried mushrooms are not available, just use fresh mushrooms, and add the sherry to the sauce after frying them.

VARIATION

Replace the chicken breast fillets with medallions of pork sliced from a tenderloin (fillet).

TECHNIQUE

Stir sufficient stock into the sauce to thin it to the desired consistency.

CHICKEN LIVERS IN MUSHROOM CUPS

Chicken livers are quick to cook and go well with bacon and mushrooms. Here livers and bacon are arranged on large flat mushrooms to make a stylish assembly. Serve with hot garlic bread or creamy mashed potato, and a crisp green vegetable or leafy salad.

SERVES 4

8 large flat mushrooms, at least 7.5 cm (3 inches) in diameter
45 ml (3 tbsp) olive oil
4 bay leaves (optional)
10 ml (2 tsp) chopped fresh or dried thyme
salt and pepper
225 g (8 oz) chicken livers
50 ml (2 fl oz) dry sherry
8 thin rashers streaky bacon, derinded
1 onion
thyme sprigs, to garnish

PREPARATION TIME
20 minutes
COOKING TIME
About 25 minutes
FREEZING
Not suitable

300 CALS PER SERVING

1. Preheat the oven to 200°C (400°F) Mark 6. Wipe the mushrooms and brush them all over generously with olive oil. Arrange cup-side up in a single layer in a well-oiled roasting tin, sitting each alternate one on a bay leaf if you like. Sprinkle the thyme and a little salt over the mushrooms.

2. Trim the chicken livers, cutting away the white fibrous tissue and any discoloured bits. Divide the livers between the mushrooms, trickle half the sherry over them and season with pepper. Cut the bacon rashers into strips and arrange over the livers in each mushroom.

3. Peel and finely chop the onion and scatter over the dish. Bake in the oven for about 25 minutes until the mushrooms are tender, by which time the livers will be cooked.

4. Transfer the mushrooms to a warmed serving dish or individual plates. Pour the remaining sherry into the roasting tin and bring to the boil, stirring and scraping up any sediment from the bottom of the tin. Pour over the mushrooms and serve immediately, garnished with thyme sprigs.

NOTE: Garlic bread wrapped in foil can be heated on a low shelf in the oven below the mushrooms.

VARIATION

Use sliced lamb's kidneys instead of chicken livers, allowing two per portion.

TECHNIQUE

Arrange the bacon strips on top of the chicken livers.

BACON, POTATO AND MUSHROOM GRATIN

A satisfyingly self-indulgent supper dish for two, simple to knock together late in the evening when you've been busy with other things. Serve with a crisp leafy salad and a glass of wine.

SERVES 2

**250 g (9 oz) small new
    potatoes**
salt and pepper
1 small onion
125 g (4 oz) bacon, derinded
30 ml (2 tbsp) olive oil
125 g (4 oz) mushrooms
125 g (4 oz) Cheddar cheese

PREPARATION TIME
5 minutes
COOKING TIME
20 minutes
FREEZING
Not suitable

595 CALS PER SERVING

1. Wash the potatoes and halve them (unless they are very small). Cook in salted water until tender. Drain thoroughly.

2. In the meantime, peel and chop the onion; dice the bacon. Heat the olive oil in a frying pan and add the onion and bacon. Cook gently, stirring frequently, to soften the onion and crisp the bacon. Meanwhile, wipe the mushrooms. Leave very small button mushrooms whole; halve or slice larger ones. Add them to the bacon towards the end of cooking and stir-cook for 2-3 minutes. Preheat the grill.

3. Transfer the bacon, onion and mushrooms to a flameproof gratin dish and stir in the potatoes. Season with pepper only, and grate the cheese all over the surface. Grill until the cheese is bubbling, then serve immediately.

NOTE: It's important to cook the diced bacon and onion slowly and to stir frequently.

VARIATION

For a vegetarian version, replace the bacon with sliced leeks, increasing the olive oil by 15 ml (1 tbsp) and adding a sprinkling of thyme.

TECHNIQUE

Add the mushrooms to the fried onion and bacon mixture towards the end of cooking and stir-cook for 2-3 minutes.

STUFFED THAI OMELETTE

For this very quick and tasty supper an omelette is used as a wrapper to parcel up pork and vegetables. For a more substantial meal, serve with rice or noodles. Alternatively, you can serve the omelette as a starter for four, accompanied by prawn crackers.

SERVES 2

1 carrot
1 small leek
1 large garlic clove
2.5 cm (1 inch) piece fresh
    root ginger
1 tomato
3 eggs
salt and pepper
45 ml (3 tbsp) vegetable oil
125 g (4 oz) minced pork
5 ml (1 tsp) soft brown
    sugar
15 ml (1 tbsp) nam pla (Thai
    fish sauce) (optional)
10-15 ml (2-3 tsp) soy sauce
5-15 ml (1-3 tsp) rice
    vinegar or cider vinegar

PREPARATION TIME
10 minutes
COOKING TIME
7-8 minutes
FREEZING
Not suitable

460 CALS PER SERVING

1. Peel and grate the carrot. Trim and finely shred the leek. Crush the garlic. Peel and grate the ginger. Skin the tomato and chop it finely.

2. In a bowl, beat the eggs together lightly, using a fork. Season with salt and pepper.

3. Heat half of the oil in a wok or frying pan. Add the pork with the garlic and ginger and fry, stirring constantly, until the pork is evenly coloured and cooked through.

4. Add the carrot and leek and stir-fry for 1 minute, then add the tomato, sugar, fish sauce if using, soy sauce and vinegar. (Use the greater quantities of soy sauce and vinegar listed if you don't have fish sauce). Season generously with pepper and stir-fry for 2-3 minutes. Transfer to a warmed dish and keep warm.

5. Wipe out the wok or frying pan, place over a moderate heat and add the remaining oil; swirl to distribute evenly. Pour in the beaten eggs, tilting the wok or pan to spread evenly.

6. When the omelette is just set but still moist, tip the filling into the middle and fold the four sides over the top to encase, like a parcel. Invert a warmed plate over the wok or pan, then invert both wok and plate to turn out the filled omelette. Serve immediately.

NOTE: If preferred, you can of course make 2 individual omelettes, cooking half the beaten eggs at a time, and divide the filling between them.

VARIATIONS

Substitute minced beef for the pork. For a vegetarian option, omit the meat altogether and replace with another vegetable, such as beansprouts.

TECHNIQUE

Fold the edges of the omelette over the filling to enclose it, like a parcel.

CHEESE SAUSAGE ON APPLE AND WATERCRESS SALAD

Based on a traditional Welsh recipe, these vegetarian sausages fry to a deep golden crust. They are served on a bed of watercress and apple salad, dressed with a walnut vinaigrette. Serve two each as a supper dish: alternatively a single sausage makes a tasty starter.

SERVES 4

125 g (4 oz) Caerphilly cheese
200 g (7 oz) fresh white breadcrumbs
2.5 ml (½ tsp) dried thyme
30 ml (2 tbsp) finely chopped fresh parsley
2 spring onions
salt and pepper
freshly grated nutmeg
2 eggs
a little milk, if necessary
45 ml (3 tbsp) plain white flour
10 ml (2 tsp) powdered mustard
oil for shallow-frying
SALAD
30 g (¾ oz) walnut halves
10 ml (2 tsp) sherry vinegar
45 ml (3 tbsp) olive oil
15 ml (1 tbsp) walnut oil
1 small red onion
50 g (2 oz) watercress
2 green eating apples

PREPARATION TIME
15 minutes
COOKING TIME
10 minutes
FREEZING
Suitable: Uncooked mixture only

705 CALS PER SERVING

1. Grate the cheese into a bowl and mix with the breadcrumbs, thyme and parsley. Trim and finely chop the spring onions and add to the mixture. Season with a little salt, and generously with pepper and nutmeg. Mix thoroughly.

2. Separate one egg, dropping the white into a shallow dish. In another bowl, beat the whole egg and egg yolk lightly together, then add to the crumb mixture and mix thoroughly. If necessary, moisten with a little milk; the mixture must be soft enough to gather into balls.

3. Prepare the salad dressing. Chop half the walnuts very finely by hand or in a food processor. Beat in the vinegar, olive and walnut oils, and seasoning.

4. Scoop the sausage mixture into 8 balls and shape each one with your hands into a cylindrical sausage. Beat the reserved egg white lightly until frothy. Mix the flour and mustard powder on a plate.

5. Heat the oil for shallow-frying in a frying pan. Brush the sausages lightly all over with egg white then, using 2 forks, roll them in the flour and mustard. Fry the sausages slowly enough to allow them to cook right through, turning frequently to ensure they brown evenly. Drain on kitchen paper.

6. Meanwhile, peel and thinly slice the onion. Trim the watercress. Quarter, core and slice the apples. Toss these ingredients together and arrange on serving plates. Drizzle with the walnut vinaigrette and sprinkle with the remaining walnuts. Serve the cheese sausages piping hot, with the salad.

NOTE: Soft white breadcrumbs are best made in a food processor from day-old bread. The dressing for the salad can be made entirely in a blender or food processor.

VARIATION

Use another sharp white cheese or a strong Cheddar in place of Caerphilly.

TECHNIQUE

Brush the sausages with egg white, then turn each one in the flour and mustard mixture to coat evenly.

RICE, TUNA AND FLAGEOLETS

Lemon, leeks and parsley, plus storecupboard standbys are all that's needed to produce this tasty supper. You could also serve it as a starter or cold as part of a buffet spread. As a starter it will serve 6.

SERVES 4

250 g (9 oz) long-grain rice
juice of 1 large lemon
salt and pepper
200 g (7 oz) trimmed leeks
100 ml (3½ fl oz) olive oil
400 g (14 oz) can flageolet
  beans
200 g (7 oz) can tuna in oil
60 ml (4 tbsp) chopped fresh
  parsley
TO SERVE
lemon wedges
parsley sprigs, to garnish

PREPARATION TIME
5-6 minutes
COOKING TIME
20-25 minutes
FREEZING
Not suitable

655 CALS PER SERVING

1. Put the rice into a saucepan with the lemon juice and 400 ml (14 fl oz) cold water. Bring to the boil, stirring. Season with salt, cover with a tight-fitting lid and reduce the heat to very low. Cook for 12 minutes, then turn off the heat and, without removing the lid, leave to stand for a further 10-15 minutes.

2. Meanwhile, finely shed the leeks. When you turn off the heat under the rice, heat half the olive oil in a frying pan. Add the leeks and cook until softened.

3. Drain the beans, rinse under cold running water and drain thoroughly. Drain and roughly flake the tuna. Add the beans and tuna to the leeks and cook just long enough to warm through. Cover and keep warm.

4. Trickle the remaining olive oil over the rice, season generously with pepper and scatter the parsley on top. Fork the rice to separate the grains, then lightly fork the leek mixture through it. Turn into a warmed bowl or pile onto warmed serving plates and place lemon wedges alongside. Garnish with parsley to serve.

NOTE: This dish can be served hot, warm or cold.

VARIATIONS

Use canned chick peas or cannellini beans instead of flageolets.

TECHNIQUE

Lightly fork the leek, tuna and bean mixture through the cooked rice.

PASTA AND COURGETTES IN TOMATO CREAM

A beautiful pink and creamy dish, combining ribbon pasta with pretty green-edged ribbons of courgettes in a creamy tomato sauce. Serve as a vegetarian starter or supper dish, accompanied by a salad if you like. Alternatively, it makes an excellent accompaniment to grilled fish, chicken or lamb.

SERVES 4

225 g (8 oz) courgettes
225 g (8 oz) tomatoes
350 g (12 oz) trenette, linguine, fettucine or other pasta
salt and pepper
25 g (1 oz) butter
150 ml (¼ pint) double cream
30 ml (2 tbsp) finely grated Parmesan cheese
small handful of fresh basil leaves, roughly torn if large

PREPARATION TIME
10 minutes
COOKING TIME
10-12 minutes
FREEZING
Not suitable

570 CALS PER SERVING

1. Using a swivel vegetable peeler, pare strips lengthways from the courgettes to make ribbons, discarding the outside skin pieces; set aside. Immerse the tomatoes in a bowl of boiling water for 30 seconds, then drain and peel away the skins. Roughly chop the tomato flesh.

2. Cook the pasta in a large pan of boiling salted water until *al dente* (tender but still firm to the bite).

3. Meanwhile, melt the butter in a pan, add the chopped tomatoes and cook gently until softened. Add the cream and season with salt and pepper. Gently stir in the courgette ribbons and simmer for about 2 minutes, until they are just soft.

4. Drain the pasta and transfer to a warmed serving bowl. Pour the sauce over the pasta and sprinkle on half of the Parmesan. Toss very gently to mix. Scatter with the remaining Parmesan and basil leaves and serve immediately.

VARIATION

Use leeks, cut in long thin strips, instead of the courgettes. Rather than cook them in the sauce, add them to the pasta for the last 2 minutes of its cooking. Drain together with the pasta and toss in the tomato cream sauce.

TECHNIQUE

Using a swivel vegetable peeler and pressing firmly, shave long strips from the courgettes to make ribbons.

Salad of Spinach and Feta Cheese

A salad of tasty dark green leaves offset with slivers of red pepper and dazzling white cubes of salty feta cheese. The hot dressing slightly wilts the leaves and takes the chill off the salad. Serve with hot French bread, or garlic and herb bread if you have time to make some.

SERVES 4

350 g (12 oz) washed young
   spinach leaves
2-3 spring onions
1 red pepper
salt and pepper
200 g (7 oz) feta cheese
2 garlic cloves
30 ml (2 tbsp) pine nuts
60 ml (4 tbsp) olive oil
30 ml (2 tbsp) wine vinegar

PREPARATION TIME
10 minutes
COOKING TIME
3-4 minutes
FREEZING
Not suitable

350 CALS PER SERVING

1. Spread the spinach leaves on individual serving plates. Trim and finely shred the spring onions. Quarter, deseed and finely slice the red pepper. Scatter these over the spinach and season with salt and pepper.

2. Cut the cheese into 1 cm (½ inch) cubes and scatter over the salads. Peel and finely chop the garlic and set aside.

3. Immediately before serving, put the pine nuts in a small heavy-based frying pan and shake over a moderate heat until they begin to colour and develop a toasted aroma.

4. Immediately add the oil and garlic to the pan and continue to shake over the heat until the garlic sizzles and begins to turn pale golden. Immediately add the wine vinegar, then pour the dressing over the salads. Serve straight away, with hot bread.

NOTE: Packets of ready-washed spinach are widely available from supermarkets. If you buy unprepared spinach, add 10 minutes to the preparation time to allow for thorough washing, picking over and drying.

VARIATION

Substitute leaves of batavia lettuce or frisée for the young spinach.

TECHNIQUE

Trim the spring onions, then slice lengthwise into long fine shreds.

HONEY-SCENTED CREAMS

This light creamy whipped dessert is particularly quick and easy to prepare. The more scented your honey, the more delicious the result – orange blossom is particularly fragrant. Alternatively, try lemon blossom, acacia or a herb-scented honey. Crisp dessert biscuits are the perfect complement.

SERVES 4

3 (size 2) eggs, chilled

75 ml (5 tbsp) scented thin
   honey

freshly grated nutmeg

150 ml (¼ pint) double
   cream

clusters of redcurrants or
   seedless green grapes, to
   decorate

PREPARATION TIME
10 minutes, plus chilling
COOKING TIME
Nil
FREEZING
Not suitable

295 CALS PER SERVING

1. Separate the eggs. In a bowl, whisk the honey with the egg yolks and nutmeg to taste until pale in colour and slightly thickened.

2. In another bowl, whisk the egg whites until they stand in firm peaks. In a separate bowl, whip the cream until thick. Stir the honey mixture into the cream until evenly blended, then fold this into the whisked egg whites. Spoon into serving glasses and chill thoroughly.

3. To serve, sprinkle a little grated nutmeg over each serving and hang a tiny cluster of redcurrants or seedless grapes over the rim of each glass. Serve with dessert biscuits.

NOTE: Honey which has set in the jar will liquefy if stood in a jug of hot water.

EGGS: 'At risk' groups including the elderly, pregnant women, babies, young children and people who have immune-deficiency disease are advised to avoid eating raw eggs, due to the possible risk of salmonella.

VARIATION

Prepare the dessert in a large glass dish if you prefer, and spoon it out at the table.

TECHNIQUE

Lightly fold the honey and cream mixture into the whisked egg whites, using a large metal spoon.

RASPBERRY PINEAU SYLLABUB

Pineau des Charentes lends a superb flavour to this refreshing syllabub. A fortified wine, it has the fragrant warmth and mellow sweetness of the Charentais melon, with whom it shares a birthplace in the Cognac region of France. Strengthed with brandy, Pineau comes in both white and rosé shades. The white – which is actually a rich gold – is better for this recipe.

SERVES 4

250 g (9 oz) raspberries
50 g (2 oz) caster sugar
300 ml (½ pint) double
    cream
125 ml (4 fl oz) Pineau des
    Charentes (see note)

PREPARATION TIME
10 minutes
COOKING TIME
Nil
FREEZING
Not suitable

430 CALS PER SERVING

1. Put two thirds of the raspberries in a large bowl and crush with a fork. Sprinkle with the sugar.

2. In a separate bowl, whip the cream until it is thick but barely holding peaks. Continue whipping as you gradually add the Pineau des Charentes.

3. Fold the wine and cream mixture into the crushed raspberries until evenly blended. Spoon into glass serving dishes and decorate with the remaining raspberries. Serve with crisp dessert biscuits.

NOTE: If Pineau des Charentes is unavailable, you could use Dubonnet instead. It will impart a different flavour, but one that complements the raspberries quite well.

VARIATION

Substitute redcurrants for half of the raspberries, using little clusters for decoration.

TECHNIQUE

Lightly fold the wine and cream mixture into the crushed raspberries, using a large metal spoon.

GALETTES OF MINTED BLACKCURRANTS

Crisply elevated layers of puff pastry flatter rich-tasting fruits, like blackcurrants. For convenience, the puff pastry can be shop-bought; it cooks quickly in a hot oven. Serve these galettes hot, accompanying by cream or yogurt streaked purple with blackcurrant liqueur.

SERVES 4

350 g (12 oz) fresh or frozen
    blackcurrants
350 g (12 oz) bought puff
    pastry
15 g (½ oz) butter
45 ml (3 tbsp) caster sugar
2 fresh mint sprigs
300 ml (½ pint) crème
    fraîche or Greek-style
    yogurt
15 ml (1 tbsp) crème de
    cassis liqueur (optional)
blackcurrant or mint leaves,
    to decorate

PREPARATION TIME
20 minutes
COOKING TIME
15-20 minutes
FREEZING
Not suitable

640 CALS PER SERVING

1. Preheat the oven to 220°C (425°F) Mark 7. Meanwhile, top and tail fresh blackcurrants or spread frozen ones out in a single layer on a tray to thaw quickly.

2. Roll out the pastry on a lightly floured surface to a 5 mm (¼ inch) thickness. Using a suitable cutter or a saucer as a guide, cut out 4 rounds, each 10 cm (4 inches) in diameter. Transfer to a baking sheet. Prick the pastry rounds with a fork, leaving a 1 cm (½ inch) margin at the edge.

3. Melt the butter and brush over the edges of the galettes. Scatter the blackcurrants over the pastry rounds, leaving the edges clear, then sprinkle half the sugar over the fruit.

4. Bake the galettes in the oven for 15-20 minutes. Meanwhile, chop the mint and mix with the remaining sugar. Spoon the crème fraîche or yogurt into a serving dish and swirl the crème de cassis through it, if using.

5. Sprinkle the minted sugar evenly over the galettes just before serving. Decorate with blackcurrant or mint leaves and serve with the flavoured crème fraîche or yogurt.

VARIATIONS

Replace the blackcurrants with gooseberries and flavour the accompanying cream with a sweet muscat wine. Alternatively, you can use rhubarb; in this case double the sugar and streak the cream with a few crushed raspberries.

TECHNIQUE

Prick the pastry rounds with a fork, leaving a 1 cm (½ inch) margin at the edge.

BANANAS GRILLED WITH CARDAMOM BUTTER

Cooking magically intensifies the flavour of bananas and transforms their flesh to a melting softness. Here the flavour is further enhanced with the most exotic of spices, and a crisply caramelised crust contrasts the soft texture. Ice cream is the perfect complement.

SERVES 4

4 large bananas, rinsed
2-3 cardamom pods
50 g (2 oz) soft dark brown
  sugar
50 g (2 oz) butter, at room
  temperature
TO SERVE
vanilla, coffee or chocolate
  ice cream (optional)

PREPARATION TIME
10 minutes
COOKING TIME
5-8 minutes, depending on size
and ripeness of bananas
FREEZING
Not suitable

280 CALS PER SERVING

1. Line the grill pan with foil, then replace the grill rack. Preheat the grill. Slit each banana skin along its length and cut the skin back a little at each end so that you can open it out slightly.

2. Break open the cardamom pods and empty the seeds into a mortar. Crush them with a pestle, adding half of the sugar in the latter stages of crushing.

3. Beat the butter and cardamom-flavoured sugar together in a bowl, then push some of the mixture along the slit in each banana.

4. Place the bananas open-side up on the grill rack and grill for 3-5 minutes until the butter melts into them and the flesh begins to soften. Sprinkle the remaining sugar on top and flash back under the grill until the bananas are soft-ened and the topping is caramelised.

5. Serve the bananas hot in their skins, with ice cream if you like.

NOTE: The buttery syrup which exudes during cooking can be spooned from the lined grill pan back over the bananas when you serve them.

VARIATIONS

Other spices, such as cinnamon or ginger, can ring the changes on cardamom, or you could use vanilla sugar.

TECHNIQUE

Insert the spiced butter into the slit bananas.

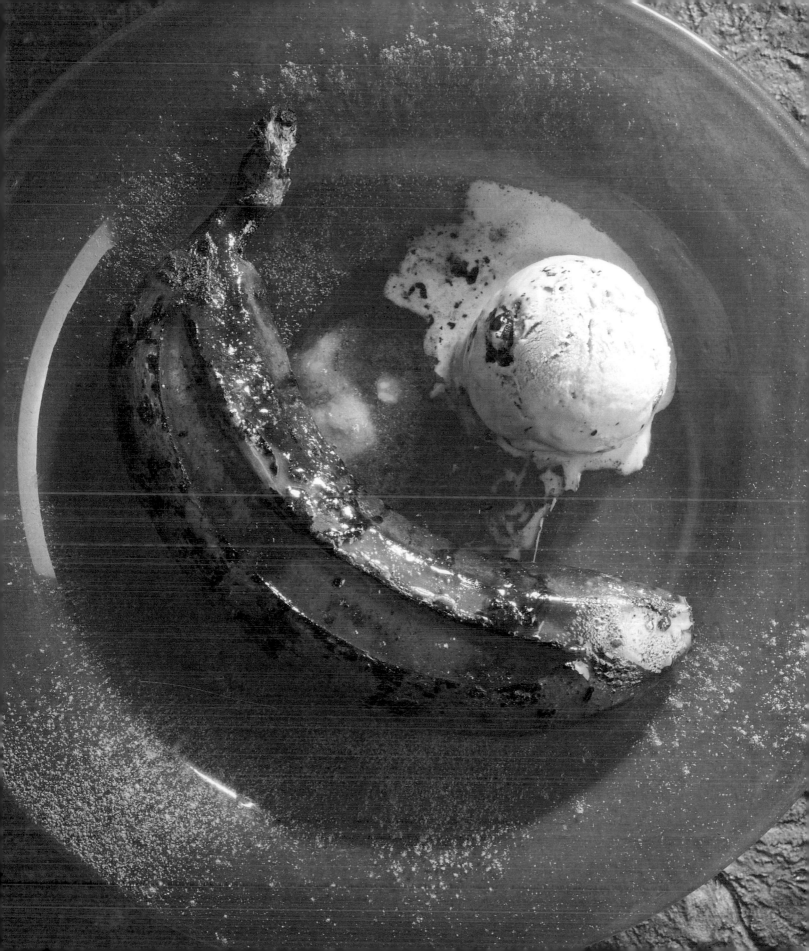

DATES AND BANANAS WITH SCENTED CREAM AND CINNAMON

Soft, sweet and romantically rose-scented, this simple fruit-based dessert has a voluptuous air of Arabian nights about it. In fact it is very quickly assembled at any time of the year!

SERVES 4

200 g (7 oz) fresh dates

200 ml (7 fl oz) whipping cream

10-15 ml (2-3 tsp) icing sugar, or to taste

2.5 ml (½ tsp) triple-strength rosewater

2 large ripe bananas

2.5 ml (½ tsp) ground cinnamon

PREPARATION TIME
10 minutes
COOKING TIME
Nil
FREEZING
Not suitable

330 CALS PER SERVING

1. Halve and stone the dates. Whip the cream until it is just thickened, but not stiff. Sweeten with icing sugar to taste and flavour with the rosewater. Chill until you are ready to serve.

2. Just before serving, peel and slice the bananas. Arrange the halved dates and banana slices on individual serving plates.

3. Spoon some of the scented cream over the fruit and sprinkle lightly with cinnamon. Serve the remaining cream in a bowl or jug.

NOTE: Don't slice the bananas until just before you are ready to serve the dessert otherwise they will discolour.

VARIATION

You can substitute yogurt or crème fraîche for the cream.

TECHNIQUE

Whip the cream until it is just thickened, but not stiff.

PEACHES WITH A HOT ZABAGLIONE SAUCE

The ripe golden fruits of high summer are at their headiest served with a frothy sweet wine sauce. Use either peaches or nectarines for this dessert, but make sure they are perfectly ripe to ensure optimum flavour.

SERVES 4

4 ripe peaches or nectarines
60 ml (4 tbsp) Marsala wine
25 g (1 oz) caster sugar
2 eggs, plus 1 extra yolk

PREPARATION TIME
5 minutes
COOKING TIME
7-8 minutes
FREEZING
Not suitable

130 CALS PER SERVING

1. Put the peaches into a heatproof bowl and pour on sufficient boiling water to cover. Leave for 1 minute, then drain and peel away the skins. Halve and stone the peaches, and arrange rounded-side up on individual plates.

2. Immediately before serving, mix the wine and sugar together in a heatproof bowl. Set the bowl over a pan of boiling water and stir gently until the sugar dissolves completely.

3. In a separate bowl, beat the eggs and extra yolk lightly together, then whisk into the hot wine mixture. Continue whisking over the boiling water until the mixture forms a thick, billowy froth.

4. Pour the hot zabaglione sauce over the peaches and serve immediately.

NOTE: A thin metal bowl is best for making zabaglione, but a heatproof glass one will do – and has the added advantage that you can lift it to see when all the liquid has been absorbed into the mounting froth.

VARIATION

When peaches and nectarines are not in season, you could use peach halves canned in natural juice.

TECHNIQUE

Continue whisking over boiling water until the zabaglione has increased in volume and is thick enough to leave a trail on the surface when the whisk is lifted.

PEARS WITH A HOT FUDGE SAUCE

A rich, gooey fudge sauce is the perfect foil for delicate slices of juicy dessert pear. For maximum contrast, chill the sliced pears before pouring on the hot sauce. Serve with a spoonful of good quality vanilla ice cream.

SERVES 4

4 large, ripe dessert pears,
   such as Comice or
   William
juice of 1 lemon
SAUCE
75 g (3 oz) butter
15 ml (1 tbsp) golden syrup
75 g (3 oz) soft brown sugar
pinch of salt
60 ml (4 tbsp) evaporated
   milk
TO SERVE
vanilla ice cream

PREPARATION TIME
10 minutes
COOKING TIME
7-8 minutes
FREEZING
Not suitable

325 CALS PER SERVING

1. Peel, halve and core the pears, then cut each half into slices. Arrange on individual serving plates and sprinkle all over with lemon juice to prevent discoloration. Chill in the refrigerator until required.

2. When you are ready to serve the dessert, put the butter, syrup, brown sugar, salt and evaporated milk in a heavy-based pan over a low heat. Stir until the sugar dissolves, then bring to the boil without further stirring.

3. Pour the hot fudge sauce over the chilled pear slices and serve immediately, with ice cream.

NOTE: Allow the sauce to cool a little before serving, especially to children.

VARIATION

The fudge sauce also makes a good topping for plain, nut or praline ice cream.

TECHNIQUE

Stir the ingredients for the hot fudge sauce in a heavy-based pan over a low heat until the sugar dissolves, then bring to the boil without further stirring.